Day Trading For Beginners

The Secrets on How to Get Rich Day Trading for Beginners

Introduction

I want to thank you and congratulate you for downloading the book, "A Beginners Guide To Day Trading: The Secrets on How To Get Rich Day Trading For Beginners".

This book helps beginners understand what day trading is, what it's all about, and how one can get rich through it.

This book is particularly helpful for people who are:

- New to the world of day trading
- Excited to find out the idea and concept behind day trading
- Willing to learn how to start day trading
- Willing to start earning money through day trading

At this point, you are probably wondering what makes this book different from other books that discuss day trading.

First, the book explains the meaning of day trading in its simplest form. It also discusses different day trading options one can avail of. It outlines what a beginner day trader should and shouldn't do to succeed in day trading.

Second, it provides tips and strategies that will be helpful for beginners so they can get the most out of their experience. It also contains helpful information on how one can start earning through day trading and what must be done to continue earning from it.

Third, the book outlines the rules that every newbie day trader must follow, as well as tips on how one can master the various day trading options.

Finally, it explains what the advantages of day trading are.

Thanks again for downloading this book, I hope you enjoy it!

Chapter I: What Is Day Trading?

Day trading is the acquisition and sale of various financial instruments within one trading day only. Day traders or active traders are the individuals engaged in day trading. On the outside looking in, it seems like a pretty decent and exciting job. Nevertheless, in order to succeed in it, one must know its ins and outs.

If one is interested in participating in day trading, one of the first things a person should know is the different types of financial instruments that can be traded. These include stock options, stocks, currencies, and interest rate futures, among others.

On top of becoming familiar with the financial instruments, an individual should also study helpful day trading strategies so that one might not get lost. An individual must remember that day trading involves more than just purchasing financial instruments. Actually, it can be complicated, so it is very vital for an aspiring day trader to be focused and committed to ensuring success for one's new venture.

What Are the Advantages of Day Trading?

Gone are the days when professional traders monopolized stock trading. Now everybody can come and go as they please, which is one big advantage of day trading. It has leveled out the playing field between amateurs and professionals. As long as you have the right system in place and know the perfect time to execute, it can be anybody's ballgame.

• The first advantage of day trading is **SPEED**. The state of the art technology used these days can greatly benefit traders because it allows them to receive and analyze price quotes in real time and directly send an execution order to the NASDAQ market maker electronically. With confirmations given in a matter of seconds, traders can get out as soon as they want to when they get what they want.

• The second advantage of day trading is **OPTIMAL CONTROL**. When you are a day trader, you are your own boss and you're not answerable to anyone because you are your own broker. You make all the decisions if you want to purchase or sell, analyze trends or scrutinize the existing financial data. There's no such thing as price slippage because these market prices are monitored the whole time. While trading, you are always aware of the best time to bid or what is the ideal ask price.

• The third advantage of day trading is **A GOOD NIGHT'S SLEEP**. That's right. You get a good nights' sleep because you always go home flat. Overnight positions are non-existent thereby minimizing the risk of exposure that usually happens overnight.

As a day trader, you know the risks, you take a chance based on the signs and signals you are reading and hope that your system will work. In times when it doesn't work, you can calmly tell yourself that you did your best, take your losses and leave. Whereas, if you have entrusted your trading to someone else who is not doing what he is supposed to while at the same time being a smart ass the entire process, you may end up banging your head against the wall. Why is that? Because you don't know who to give the whack in the head to – the lousy broker or yourself – for allowing him to throw your money down the drain.

Knowing the advantages of a day trader will definitely encourage more people to participate in this once "restricted" industry. Nevertheless, it's not as easy as it sounds. You need to arm yourself with the right education if you want to make it big. It's easier to do that now because there are many online resources you can take advantage of.

Day trading courses will help you greatly in making sound decisions in purchasing and selling. If you come across some information about software that can do all the thinking for you, dump it. Moreover, take time to join forums and ask advice from professional traders. Seasoned traders will be more than willing to serve as your mentor and you can learn from their experiences to determine which strategies can best be applied in your favor. In addition, take note of their worst decisions that have become their biggest downfall and make sure you don't repeat after them.

Do these long enough and soon you'll be trading with ease and can even sometimes predict what's going to happen next based on the trends. Learn to read the signals and have the guts to go with what you think is right, because when you are a day trader, you have no one to rely on but yourself.

Because you're new to the exciting world of day trading, you need to be aware of its dos and don'ts. Indeed, just like in any venture, you can't go into day trading while treading on thin ice. You need to arm yourself with a head full of knowledge. In the next chapter, you will learn what you should and shouldn't do when it comes to day trading.

Chapter II: Do's and Don'ts of Day Trading for Beginners

Despite the technicality and high-strung lingo that tend to intimidate a newbie, day trading for beginners isn't really that complicated as long as you dedicate some time trying to understand the whole process. As with any endeavor, chances of failure can be placed at a minimum when you are armed with the right information and strategy to succeed.

Therefore, here are some helpful tips to help you navigate through day trading for beginners:

Understand What Day Trading Is All About

In here bonds, stocks, and other financial assets are bought and sold throughout the day using a particular system. All items purchased correspond to the sales. Profits or deficits can be seen through the discrepancies between the goods and their trade prices. The concept of day trading is to be able to finish all your transactions before the day ends so you can be sure that the closing price of your goods will remain the same. Bear in mind that changes normally occur at night.

Take This Seriously, Especially When You're Just Starting Out

Don't get carried away by the simplicity of day trading principles. Do not make foolish assumptions because this is how you will lose a lot of money. Take calculated risks if you must but do not rely merely on your guts, carefully study what's going on throughout the day to avoid hasty decisions you will soon regret.

Know What to Do Each Time You Lose

It's impossible to engage in day trading and not encounter losses once in a while. The important thing is you know how you regain these losses. Do not dwell on the past but remember not to commit the same mistakes again that cost you so much in the first place.

Make a positive change then move on.

Just Go with the Flow

Don't go against the grain. Day trading is like cutting meat, if you go against the grain, it's doubly hard to cut through, and when you're not careful, may destroy it all together. Consider this especially if you're still a novice feeling your way through. Concentrate on stocks that are high selling and sell those that aren't. This is because these stocks usually rise and develop and when you use this strategy, you are on the safe side.

Keep Your Cool and Be Objective

Day trading for beginners entails that you always keep your cool and try to be objective during the entire course. It's normal for emotions to run high especially during the rise and fall of these stocks throughout the day, but be calm. Do not let your emotions get the better of you that may result in faulty trading decisions. Assess the situation carefully and do not panic. Instead, review where you have gone wrong and pick it up from there. Be open and flexible so it will be easy for you to shift gears when necessary.

Patience Is a Requirement, Not Just a Virtue

Things do not always go the way you want or expect them to, at least not right away. So be patient until you appropriately reach certain points. It takes time and practice for you to learn the signs on how to know when a specific item already reaches the peak price.

Day trading is not for everyone. If you are impatient and gets easily frustrated, perhaps this endeavor is not cut out for you. However, for those who are willing to persevere and take the fall every now and then, the pay-off in the financial trading market is very much rewarding. Continuously look for better methods and strategies for reading the signals when to buy and sell, and learn the intricacies of the trade by joining online forums and finding other useful resources. Before you know it, you'll be trading like a pro.

Of course, in order to start trading like a pro, you need to be aware of the pitfalls and snares you need to avoid. The next chapter dishes out the highs and lows.

Chapter III: Important Day Trading Rules to Follow to Avoid Pitfalls

You will not last long if you rely solely on marketing strategies, risk management, chart patterns, or technical analysis. You have to go beyond the technical aspects of day trading if you want to reap optimum results consistently. One thing that people don't realize is that this is a profession, and as with any profession, you need to exert a certain amount of effort to surpass the learning curve. Other than that, there are some important trading rules to follow in order to avoid pitfalls.

The worst mistake you can do is join day trading as if you're merely joining the lottery, you're just waiting it out until some miracle happens and you reap a truckload of money. It doesn't work out that way. You need to have the right kind of attitude, have discipline and self-control for you to thrive and not just survive. All the books you've read about the stock market, all the online resources, and forums you have joined to gain insight about day trading rules and strategies will do you no good if you do not strike the perfect balance between your thoughts and emotions.

Here are some helpful day trading rules to follow for both amateurs and pros:

Have a Consistent Frame of Mind

No, you cannot expect the market to be consistent since it is in a highly volatile environment and things always turn out the way you expect them to. The trick is to be able to adapt, think quickly, and execute the right moves so you won't be left behind. Know how to read the probability scenario because this can give you leverage. Once you've mastered how to handle these probability set-ups, you'll know the perfect timing for trading.

Keep Your Cool, Don't Overtrade

This is a common mistake mostly done by beginners. Learn to keep your cool because when you get too excited you commit the deadliest sins in trading. You need to be patient and wait it out until you are sure that the right moment has come for you to strike. Your gains and losses will highly depend on your ability to control yourself.

Focus So You Won't Get Derailed

Everybody knows risks are involved and huge amounts of money are at stake in day trading. However, these risks can be placed at a minimum if you follow tried and tested rules in trading. It's alright to shift gears once in a while to see if what the successful pros are doing can also work for you, but don't do this too often. Remember, they've been doing this for years and they know exactly what they are getting themselves into. However, for you, the more you experiment, the more money you're going to lose.

Never Force Yourself to Trade if You Are Not Up For It

You cannot make instantaneous decisions if you are not in the right frame of mind, haven't gotten any sleep or having an anxiety attack. It's simply not worth the risk. Trade only when you are physically, mentally and emotionally equipped to do so.

Use a Trading Log to Your Advantage

Majority of traders find this unnecessary but they are wrong. Not only must you log every trade you must also jot down your thoughts and emotions during the entire process. Compare your wins and losses. What state of mind where you in when you were winning, consequently, what were eating you emotionally or troubling you mentally when you suffered all those losses? Next time you'll have a better idea what to do.

Clearly, there's not one perfect strategy that will work for everybody. Each trader must learn how to come up with the most effective day trading rules that can benefit him or her the most.

Chapter IV: Sure-Fire Day Trading Tips for the Amateurs and Pros

When it comes to day trading for both amateurs and professionals, here's one thing you need to know: there is nothing, not even the thinnest line, which separates the two. Some professional traders have been doing this for years and yet commit the same mistakes over and over again. On the other hand, an awful lot of newbie traders go by some strict rules and hit the jackpot on the first few tries. There is really no concoction to come up with sure-fire trading tips, rather it's really a matter of careful analyzing and perfect timing to make it big in day trading.

Therefore, here are some day trading tips tried and tested by both amateurs and pros alike:

Large Trades vs. Small Trades

Don't be too impulsive and let it get the best of you. Self-control is essential to prevent you from trading randomly and missing all the right trades that will surely come your way had you been patient enough. You must develop a system that allows you to identify the best trade of the day before you take the plunge. Trade not more than twice a day. Bear in mind that it is better to focus on a few large trades than on plenty of small ones if you want to be successful and profit consistently on a long-term basis.

Never Trade when you are in a Lousy Mood

This is one of the most important yet neglected day trading tips. When you are feeling lousy, you are sure to attract negative vibes that is a definite a no-no in day trading. Make sure you don't trade when you are angry, tired or feeling lousy. It is simply impossible to come up with quick and good decisions unless you are equipped physically, mentally, and psychologically to do so. Forcing the issue will only cause you a mountain of regret and a lot of wasted money.

Trade Like the Gambler

Have you heard of Kenny Rogers' song with the line that goes, "You got to know when to hold up, know when to fold up, know when to walk away, know when to run"? The words hold true in day trading. The minute you see the red flag run as fast as you can. There is a time when bold becomes stupid because you don't know your limits. There's no point keeping all those stocks for long periods of time, when you reach the perfect timing be ready to sell. On the other hand, if you see the tide turning against you, let it be. It's not the end of the world. You can always come back and trade the following day.

Know the Right Time to Trade

Many traders claim success if you trade when a new trend has just begun, or it has already run its entire course. Never trade when you're right in the middle because you have no idea what's going to happen next.

Learn from other People's Mistakes

Take in as much information as you can. Look for online resources, or better yet, join forums with other traders. Learn from their mistakes and be careful not to repeat them. Consequently, take note of the effective strategies that gave them success.

Don't Give up too Easily

The trouble with so many day traders especially with beginners is they easily give up once the volatility and unpredictability of the market takes its toll on them. As mentioned previously things don't always turn out the way you want them too. You win some; you lose some. That's just the way it is. Do not be too impatient or refuse to accept failure from time to time, because this is the only way to win in this endeavor.

The above-mentioned tips and tricks apply to both professionals and amateur day traders, but that doesn't mean there aren't tips that apply solely to beginners. After all, this is what this book is all about.

In the next chapter, we will look at some tips and tricks that day trading 'dummies' should never forget.

Chapter V: Simple Tips and Tricks to Bear in Mind When Day Trading for dummies

These days, day trading for 'dummies' (read: beginners) is not as difficult as it used to because there are tons of online resources you can use before venturing into it. However, there are basic rules you need to apply for you not to get off-track. If you have tried this before and only tasted failure, perhaps you were not able to apply all the basic rules of stock trading. Regardless whether it's long term trading or online day stock trading you want to pursue, some important principles need to be kept in mind to ensure that not all your money will go down the drain.

Day Trading for Dummies

Obviously, the term does not mean to insult your intelligence in any way. Dummies simply mean the rest of the world not really onto stocks or investment on a professional level, or those who wish to learn but have no idea where to start.

So first off, we go back to basics. Try to recall what day trading is exactly about. You may have noticed that investing and trading are used interchangeably, and that is because they are very similar in nature. Their main difference lies on the duration. Stock trading is done on a shorter term and focuses on the smaller market trends that are within the bounds of larger market movements, whereas when you talk about investing it's usually on a long-term basis.

When you're trading stocks, they never get to "sleep" which can sometimes happen when you're doing investments. Here's a quick look on what that means:

Buy 200 Shares of QRS Company at Monday's Open

Sell 200 Shares of QRS Company at Friday's Close

This is just a mock example and not a real stock trading that took place. This example is one that lasted for a week. Using the same fictitious company below is a stock day trading example:

Buy 200 Shares of QRS Company at Monday's Open

Sell 200 Shares of QRS Company at Monday's Close

As evident in both examples, the trade was opened with a buy order and was closed using a sell order. In these cases, you chose to extend. The second example is considered a stock trade simply because the position was opened and closed on the same trading day. Many stock day traders put a higher frequency on trading that happens during the day.

In addition, note that both of these examples gave the exact quantity that was traded and closed. Bear in mind that you close the trade by using the stock quantity that you opened it with, that is, if you want to be totally out of trade. This is the only way that there will not be any open positions against you.

Deciding On Your Capital

The amount of capital is another important issue you have to decide on when doing stock trading because these stocks vary significantly. It is not that difficult to open as standard brokerage because you will just need about five hundred to a thousand dollars to begin. However if they begin to classify you as a pattern day trader you may be required to pay higher. These people are involved in more than four-day trades within a period of five trading days. If this is the case then your stock brokerages will ask you to maintain a balance of at least twenty five thousand dollars in your account. This can still go up or vary and will depend greatly on the online stockbroker you choose to deal with.

Day trading for dummies need not be too overwhelming or complicated as long as you have the right attitude to learn the basic rules and strategies for it to be greatly rewarding and profitable.

Chapter VI: Effective Day Trading Strategies to Live By

Since today's market is increasingly volatile, surviving in stock trading will depend on the kind of trading system you set up for yourself. Any seasoned stock trader will tell you that there is not one foolproof way to protect you from losing money in this daily trade. Regardless whether you choose to follow complex or simple rules is entirely up to you because neither can guarantee profitability. Day trading strategies especially for beginners are often hit-and-miss, and through time, you will acquire the skills to read signals on the perfect timing of when to purchase and when to sell.

In order for you to succeed in day trading, you need to keep several strategies in mind. Keep these close to your heart and consider it your day trading mantras of sorts.

Day Trading Courses

Don't believe everything they tell you completely. Yes, it's helpful and convenient to have a piece of software to help you out in the trading game, but don't allow this to do all the thinking for you. It may give you an objective view on how to go about your day trading but this is not supposed to stop you from personally analyzing and studying what is actually happening with your trading throughout the day.

Review Your Mistakes

As the saying goes, "You win some, you lose some". So when the latter happens, take time to go back and review your mistakes so it won't happen again. If you trace your steps and find out exactly what went wrong, you will be able to anticipate similar scenarios in the future and avoid committing the same mistakes. This is crucial if you really want to become a successful day trader.

When Common Sense Become Uncommon

You may have noticed that common sense has, ironically, become quite uncommon these days. The most basic and simple rules are sometimes by far the hardest to live by. For example, everyone knows if you want to succeed in any kind of endeavor and not just stock trading you need to be willing to put in the long hours, have superb work ethic, have a thorough understanding about risk and money management, among others. The problem with today's trading system is that everybody is looking for the shortcut, expecting to get big bucks with so little effort. It simply does not work out that way.

So exactly what is the best way to make decisions? Make informed decisions. Don't let emotions like fear or anxiety get in the way of coming up with smart choices. This is the reason why you must invest on education. Online resources, forums, books, research on the latest trends, tools and strategies about trading and investment, any useful information you can get your hands on can be of great help.

Get the Best of Both Worlds

It's perfectly alright to learn via the hit-and-miss tactic, this way you will learn first-hand what works and what doesn't. Eventually you can predict certain events before they even take place. It may take years before you can master this but many experienced traders claim this is the best way to go. Another way is to look for a mentor who has been there and done that and came out very successful. His insights may save you time, money, and future headaches. On the other hand, you can choose to do both.

There is no perfect formula to concoct day trading strategies to reap you millions of dollars in your lifetime. Trading is like gambling, if you don't play, you don't win. You must learn how to embrace losses as gracefully as you do success. Only those who are willing to

take risks and sacrifice have a good
chance of striking it big.

So far, you've discovered the
following:

- What day trading means

- What it's all about

- What tips and tricks you need to
learn

- What strategies you need to employ

- What pitfalls to avoid

Now that you know the above-
mentioned, it's right about time to find
out what you should do in case there's a
market decline.

Chapter VII: More Advanced Strategies For Day Trading

Experienced day traders can attest to the fact that day trading stocks is greatly affected during market declines. For the main reason that the market becomes highly unpredictable during these declines regardless whether it's short term or the usual bear market. This unpredictability can eat off the capital of the most seasoned traders if their trading is not adjusted.

Volatility during the Bear Markets

Take note that there will always be major pullbacks as an aftermath of the increase in stock prices. This unpredictability in day trading stocks can change the market's direction and each trader must know this lest he be caught unaware.

Knowing that the possibility of this conditions occurring is very real, what must day traders do to protect themselves? First, they must be keen on looking for clues or indicators that will give them a good idea where the direction of the market is headed. Among these indicators are the TRIN, the advance/decline line, New 52 week highs and lows, among others.

Learn When to Switch Gears Fast While You Still Can

You may have to switch tactics in managing your trade when you know that it has turned out into a bear market. The primary concern being the increase in market unpredictability, traders must consider changing their position size. If you're used to trading a thousand shares in a single stock during bull season, five hundred will work better for you during bear season. Newbies will feel they're losing a lot of money when doing these smaller types of trading, while the seasoned pros know that self-preservation is more important for times when the market is a lot safer.

The Danger of Overnight Reversals

Another major concern of day traders are the reversals of the market within the day during bear markets that makes them more vulnerable to large openings. Not all day traders close during the day, and therefore, those that carry overnight positions are highly at risk of reversals in the market. If they choose to maintain these positions overnight, it might be wise to decrease it should there be a reversal overnight.

Bear in mind that the market tendency in the end will be for trading of stocks to increase each day. Therefore, even when the market is on the lower trends, there will still be days when it will close on the upside. Remember that during current down move, almost forty percent of these trading days closed on the upside. Day traders therefore must learn to recognize when to take advantage of good profit opportunities when the downtrend resumes in the market after brief pauses.

Take On Other Vehicles As Well

Day traders must also take into consideration the idea of trading ETFs or stock index features that increases when the stock market falls. Profits or losses are not the only concerns but the cost of the trades as well. This is because it is more expensive for the trader to short a stock. You cannot pay the interest on those shares and sell the stock short unless you borrow these shares from your brokers first.

The Long and Short of Day Trading Stocks

Day trading stocks can still be profitable during the bear markets; however, these pitfalls must be avoided at all costs if you do not want all that money to go down the drain. Novice day traders are strongly advised not to take the plunge and just closely observe first how the professional traders do it. When they have mastered how to handle the entire

process only then can they be bold
enough to make the right move.

Chapter VIII: How to Master Your Day Trading Options

Now that you have learned most of the things you need to know in order to start day trading, it's time to review your day trading options before entering so you can avoid losing money in the process. When done correctly, day trading can be highly profitable, so if you want to pursue this endeavor for longer terms first review some key elements of trading.

Invest in a Good Education

The only way you can safely navigate through your day trading options is if you are armed with the right kind of information such as marketing strategies. Never allow trading software to do all the thinking for you without you understanding the terminologies and methods used when trading. There are candle charts that you must learn to read, you must know the difference between a put option and a call option, as well as be familiar with your risk profiles. It is also essential that you know a bit about trading psychology so you can avoid impulsive trading without careful analysis of your situation. It is therefore essential that you know exactly what you are doing before you begin.

Take Things Slowly but Surely

Perhaps some of your friends have been doing day trading for quite some time and they have been very successful at it. They have put in a lot of money and they tell you it was definitely worth it. So now, you may be tempted to bet all your money on what you think will have huge returns. Snap out of it before you run through a brick wall. If you are doing this for the first time, it's best that you take things in stride. To get a feel of how things work contact brokers that offer practice accounts using virtual money to find out if your trading strategies will work out in the real world.

When you're done practicing, you can now start on small accounts that are not too complex for your level. Ask your brokers if they have starter platforms that you can try out before you go and mingle with the major traders.

Choose a Trading Platform that Works Best for You

Different platforms have different capabilities that will greatly affect your day trading options so pick those that offer the best choices. Don't force yourself to go with platforms that are used by professional traders. These may have worked for them because years of experience have allowed them to master them well but for you it may only mean expensive mistakes one after the other. Check out each platform's charting capabilities, support and usability, charges, and other perks such as forums, coaching, and others.

After a significant amount of time gaining experience and carefully analyzing the market, you can now move up a couple of notches to look for options that can give you the highest return of investments. Some of them are as follows:

The Binary Option Market

Given the extreme volatility nature of dips and spikes of price options in trading, you cannot expect that you will get consistent results. If you are really looking for the highest ROI then this element must be seriously taken into consideration. Thus, binaries are good options.

The Short Day Trading Holding Period

The good thing about binaries is you can determine the trades' outcome at very short periods, usually within the day so there's no need to wait anxiously for the results. You will know in one hour if you can make 70% on a trade. This is the reason why so many people choose day trading binary options because they get results fast consistently with the highest

Conclusion

Day trading can be profitable as long as you familiarize yourself with its ins and outs. Remember, you'll be entering this field with money involved, and the last thing you want is to see all your hard-earned money go to waste. The idea is to grow your money and not lose it.

After learning the tips and strategies you need to follow to succeed, the pitfalls you need to avoid, and the vast options available to you, it's time to put everything into practice. The important thing now is to know how to play your cards right to get the highest return of investment.

www.ingramcontent.com/pod-product-compliance
Lightning Source LLC
Chambersburg PA
CBHW070413190526
45169CB00003B/1243